The following checklist contai
Level G of VOCABULARY WORKSI
Booklet. When you have mast
a check (✓) in front of it.

___ abject
___ abrogate
___ abstruse
___ acclamation
___ accost
___ acquisitive
___ acuity
___ aesthetic
___ affront
___ agnostic
___ allay
___ allege
___ ambient
___ amenity
___ animadversion
___ aperture
___ arrant
___ arrogate
___ askance
___ asperity
___ atrophy
___ attenuate
___ avid

___ badinage
___ banal
___ bastion
___ beatific
___ behemoth
___ belabor
___ benign
___ bestial
___ blandishment
___ brackish
___ bucolic
___ burnish

___ cabal
___ cacophonous
___ calumniate
___ canard
___ captious
___ carping
___ cavil
___ cavort
___ celerity
___ charlatan
___ chary
___ chicanery
___ cognizant
___ coherent
___ collusion
___ complicity
___ conciliate
___ concord
___ congeal
___ consign
___ consummate
___ contrite
___ convivial
___ coterie
___ countermand
___ counterpart
___ coup
___ credence
___ cynosure

___ decimate
___ decorous
___ decry
___ defunct
___ deign
___ delectable
___ delineate
___ demur
___ depraved
___ deprecate
___ derelict
___ desiccated
___ detritus
___ devious
___ diatribe
___ dilettante
___ disarray
___ discomfit
___ dissemble
___ dissidence
___ distraught

___ ebullient
___ echelon
___ eclectic
___ efficacy
___ effigy
___ effrontery
___ embellish
___ emulate
___ encomium
___ enervate
___ engender
___ ephemeral
___ epicurean
___ equity
___ eschew
___ esoteric
___ espouse
___ ethereal
___ eulogy
___ euphemism
___ evince
___ exacerbate
___ exhume
___ exigency

___ facade
___ fatuous
___ febrile
___ feckless
___ fecund
___ felicitous
___ fetish
___ fiat
___ figment
___ flaccid
___ flotsam
___ foible
___ forgo
___ fraught
___ frenetic
___ furtive

___ gainsay
___ gambit
___ garish
___ garner
___ germane
___ ghoulish
___ glean
___ gregarious
___ grouse

___ halcyon
___ hallow
___ hapless
___ histrionic

___ idiosyncrasy
___ ignominy
___ illusory
___ imminent
___ impeccable
___ impecunious
___ imperturbable
___ importune
___ improvident
___ inane
___ incarcerate
___ incendiary
___ incongruous
___ increment
___ incumbent
___ indictment
___ indigent
___ indubitable
___ inexorable
___ iniquity
___ innate
___ inordinate
___ insatiable
___ intermittent
___ interpolate
___ intransigent
___ inure
___ invidious
___ inviolable
___ irrefutable
___ irreparable

___ jettison
___ jocular
___ juggernaut

___ lackadaisical
___ laconic
___ languish
___ largesse
___ litany
___ loath
___ ludicrous
___ luminous

___ macabre
___ machination
___ maelstrom
___ mandate
___ manifest
___ mendacious
___ mesmerize
___ minutiae
___ misanthrope
___ moot
___ moratorium
___ mordant
___ moribund
___ motif
___ mundane
___ murky
___ mutable
___ myopic

___ nadir
___ nascent
___ necromancer
___ nefarious

___ neophyte
___ nettle
___ nostrum
___ nuance

___ obeisance
___ obsequious
___ obtuse
___ omnipresent
___ onerous
___ opprobrium
___ oscillate
___ overt
___ overweening

___ paltry
___ panegyric
___ pariah
___ paroxysm
___ paucity
___ pecuniary
___ pedantry
___ pejorative
___ penchant
___ penitent
___ peregrination
___ peremptory
___ perfunctory
___ perspicacity
___ pertinacious
___ picayune
___ pillory
___ piquant
___ pittance
___ plaintive
___ plenary

___ portend
___ presage
___ primordial
___ progeny
___ promulgate
___ propinquity
___ propriety
___ pusillanimous
___ putative

___ raiment
___ raze
___ rebuff
___ recant
___ reconnaissance
___ reconnoiter
___ rectitude
___ recumbent
___ redolent
___ refulgent
___ reputed
___ requite
___ restive
___ rife
___ rudiments

___ sacrilege
___ saturate
___ saturnine
___ sequester
___ seraphic
___ shambles
___ shibboleth
___ slough
___ sophistry
___ sporadic

___ stratagem
___ subsist
___ substantiate
___ substantive
___ summarily
___ sumptuous
___ suppliant
___ surveillance
___ sylvan

___ taciturn
___ talisman
___ tantamount
___ temporize
___ tenable
___ testy
___ travesty
___ tyro

___ ubiquitous
___ undulate
___ unremitting
___ unwonted
___ utopian

___ vacillate
___ verbiage
___ verdant
___ viscous
___ visionary
___ vituperative

___ winnow
___ wizened

Name ______________________________

Class ______________ Date ______________ Score ______________

I. Pronunciation *Each of the following words has been divided into syllables. Place the major stress mark (′) after the syllable that is accented when the word is pronounced.*

EXAMPLE: en er vate ⟶ **en′ er vate**

1. lack a dai si cal

2. es pouse

3. in ter mit tent

4. pro pin qui ty

II. Part of Speech *In each of the following groups, circle the item that indicates the part of speech of the word given.*

5. eschew
a. pronoun **b.** verb **c.** adverb **d.** noun

6. cynosure
a. conjunction **b.** adjective **c.** noun **d.** verb

7. abject
a. verb **b.** noun **c.** preposition **d.** adjective

III. Spelling *Circle the word that is incorrectly spelled in each of the following groups. Then supply the correct spelling in the space given.*

8. animaversion paroxysm effigy ______________

9. nadir chickanery unwonted ______________

10. consummate nascent alledge ______________

IV. Definition *From the list of words given below, choose the item that corresponds to each of the following definitions. Write it in the space given.*

incendiary	**penchant**	**arrogate**
oscillate	**imperturbable**	**epicurean**

11. to claim or take without right ______________

12. not easily excited; emotionally steady ______________

13. devoted to the pursuit of pleasure; with discriminating tastes ______________

14. a strong attraction or inclination ______________

V. Synonym *In each of the following groups, circle the item that means the same as the **boldface** word in the introductory phrase.*

15. abrogate the treaty
a. ratify **b.** annul **c.** enforce **d.** sign

16. an **incongruous** remark
a. courteous **b.** jarring **c.** lengthy **d.** scholarly

17. histrionic behavior
a. melodramatic **b.** proper **c.** subdued **d.** strange

18. surprised by their **perspicacity**
a. discernment **b.** betrayal **c.** obtuseness **d.** foolishness

---

VI. Antonym *In each of the following groups, circle the item that means the opposite of the **boldface** word in the introductory phrase.*

19. incarcerate the convict
a. trap **b.** release **c.** study **d.** imprison

20. nettle the teacher
a. irritate **b.** visit **c.** please **d.** appoint

21. a **benign** influence
a. surprising **b.** salutary **c.** negligible **d.** malevolent

22. murky water
a. clear **b.** polluted **c.** shallow **d.** salty

VII. Completing the Sentence *From the list of words given below, choose the item that best completes each of the following sentences. Write it in the space given.*

saturate	**dissemble**	**necromancer**
felicitous	**travesty**	**cognizant**

23. The torrential rain completely ____________________ the field, making it unfit for play.

24. Though I am ____________________ of the problems that we face, I am sure that with effort and persistence, we can overcome them.

25. Critics labeled the hearing a "kangaroo court" and branded its findings a "____________________ of justice."

Name ____________________

Class ____________ Date ____________ Score ____________

I. Pronunciation *Each of the following words has been divided into syllables. Place the major stress mark (′) after the syllable that is accented when the word is pronounced.*

EXAMPLE: in vid i ous → **in vid′ i ous**

1. em u late

2. re con nais sance

3. es chew

4. co her ent

II. Part of Speech *In each of the following groups, circle the item that indicates the part of speech of the word given.*

5. encomium
a. adjective **b.** noun **c.** adverb **d.** verb

6. insatiable
a. verb **b.** preposition **c.** noun **d.** adjective

7. temporize
a. noun **b.** adjective **c.** verb **d.** conjunction

III. Spelling *Circle the word that is incorrectly spelled in each of the following groups. Then supply the correct spelling in the space given.*

8. tacitern germane largesse ____________

9. tenable aquisitive substantiate ____________

10. arrogate intransigent congeel ____________

IV. Definition *From the list of words given below, choose the item that corresponds to each of the following definitions. Write it in the space given.*

coherent **belabor** **invidious**
reconnaissance **banal** **temporize**

11. having clarity ____________

12. to work on excessively; to thrash soundly ____________

13. to stall or act evasively in order to gain time or postpone a decision ____________

14. offensive, hateful, causing bitterness ____________

V. Synonym *In each of the following groups, circle the item that means the same as the* ***boldface*** *word in the introductory phrase.*

15. tired of their **carping**
a. nit-picking **b.** antics **c.** excuses **d.** incompetence

16. **banal** lyrics
a. sentimental **b.** trite **c.** humorous **d.** effective

17. **arrogate** a right
a. desire **b.** waive **c.** expropriate **d.** defend

18. an **intransigent** opponent
a. weak **b.** temporary **c.** versatile **d.** unyielding

VI. Antonym *In each of the following groups, circle the item that means the opposite of the* ***boldface*** *word in the introductory phrase.*

19. **germane** comments
a. harsh **b.** irrelevant **c.** apt **d.** recent

20. a **coherent** account
a. lengthy **b.** humorous **c.** muddled **d.** clear

21. a speech filled with **encomiums**
a. platitudes **b.** wisdom **c.** criticisms **d.** praise

22. **eschew** easy solutions
a. shun **b.** avoid **c.** condemn **d.** embrace

VII. Completing the Sentence *From the list of words given below, choose the item that best completes each of the following sentences. Write it in the space given.*

temporize	**substantiate**	**tenable**
coherent	**invidious**	**largesse**

23. Thanks to the ____________________ of alumni and corporate benefactors, the college raised enough money to build a new science center.

24. When the major saw that his position was no longer ____________________, he ordered his unit to withdraw to more defensible ground.

25. People who itemize deductions on their income tax forms must keep careful records and receipts to ____________________ their claims.

Name ______________________________

Class ______________ Date ______________ Score ______________

I. Pronunciation *Each of the following words has been divided into syllables. Place the major stress mark (′) after the syllable that is accented when the word is pronounced.*

EXAMPLE: un du late → **un′ du late**

1. ce ler i ty

2. ac cost

3. sup pli ant

4. his tri on ic

II. Part of Speech *In each of the following groups, circle the item that indicates the part of speech of the word given.*

5. undulate
a. noun **b.** verb **c.** adverb **d.** adjective

6. brackish
a. conjunction **b.** adverb **c.** verb **d.** adjective

7. sacrilege
a. adjective **b.** preposition **c.** noun **d.** verb

III. Spelling *Circle the word that is incorrectly spelled in each of the following groups. Then supply the correct spelling in the space given.*

8. maelstrom pejorative animaversion ______________

9. tallisman incendiary gambit ______________

10. avid halcion devious ______________

IV. Definition *From the list of words given below, choose the item that corresponds to each of the following definitions. Write it in the space given.*

summarily	**propriety**	**undulate**
celerity	**suppliant**	**myopic**

11. without delay or formality ______________

12. the state of being proper; standards of what is proper or socially acceptable ______________

13. swiftness, rapidity of motion or action ______________

14. to move in waves or in a wavelike fashion ______________

V. Synonym *In each of the following groups, circle the item that means the same as the* ***boldface*** *word in the introductory phrase.*

15. a legislative **gambit**
a. session **b.** right **c.** maneuver **d.** concern

16. **overt** hostility
a. concealed **b.** open **c.** unwarranted **d.** recent

17. a **pejorative** connotation
a. neutral **b.** favorable **c.** ambiguous **d.** derogatory

18. move with **celerity**
a. promptness **b.** sluggishness **c.** furtiveness **d.** emptiness

---

VI. Antonym *In each of the following groups, circle the item that means the opposite of the* ***boldface*** *word in the introductory phrase.*

19. a **myopic** approach to the problem
a. farsighted **b.** fallacious **c.** conventional **d.** shortsighted

20. **histrionic** behavior
a. irrational **b.** subdued **c.** outrageous **d.** puzzling

21. a **devious** answer
a. tricky **b.** roundabout **c.** straightforward **d.** incorrect

22. an **avid** jogger
a. elderly **b.** injured **c.** experienced **d.** reluctant

---

VII. Completing the Sentence *From the list of words given below, choose the item that best completes each of the following sentences. Write it in the space given.*

talisman	**propriety**	**undulate**
accost	**maelstrom**	**incendiary**

23. I was walking down the street when a panhandler ____________________ me with a request for a "small loan."

24. Edgar Allan Poe's story "Descent into the ____________________" tells of a shipwrecked sailor who is sucked into a huge whirlpool.

25. Police uncovered the arson ring when they stumbled across a cache of ____________________ devices in the home of one of the suspects.

Name ______________________________

Class ____________ Date ____________ Score ____________

I. Pronunciation *Each of the following words has been divided into syllables. Place the major stress mark (′) after the syllable that is accented when the word is pronounced.*

EXAMPLE: ne far i ous ⟶ **ne far′ i ous**

1. un won ted

2. ver dant

3. e vince

4. pro pin qui ty

II. Part of Speech *In each of the following groups, circle the item that indicates the part of speech of the word given.*

5. nefarious
a. verb **b.** adjective **c.** adverb **d.** noun

6. cavort
a. pronoun **b.** adverb **c.** verb **d.** conjunction

7. verbiage
a. preposition **b.** verb **c.** adjective **d.** noun

III. Spelling *Circle the word that is incorrectly spelled in each of the following groups. Then supply the correct spelling in the space given.*

8. viscuos murky feckless ____________

9. decry exhume peakant ____________

10. eulogy distraut primordial ____________

IV. Definition *From the list of words given below, choose the item that corresponds to each of the following definitions. Write it in the space given.*

evince **credence** **substantive**
propinquity **utopian** **dissemble**

11. belief, mental acceptance ____________

12. founded upon or involving a visionary view of an ideal world; impractical ____________

13. nearness in place or time; kinship ____________

14. to disguise or conceal ____________

V. Synonym *In each of the following groups, circle the item that means the same as the **boldface** word in the introductory phrase.*

15. a **viscous** substance
a. runny **b.** saline **c.** gelatinous **d.** unusable

16. a **feckless** assistant
a. dishonest **b.** able **c.** ineffective **d.** meticulous

17. **nefarious** practices
a. wicked **b.** ancient **c.** widespread **d.** commendable

18. a **verdant** landscape
a. rocky **b.** green **c.** arid **d.** snowy

VI. Antonym *In each of the following groups, circle the item that means the opposite of the **boldface** word in the introductory phrase.*

19. a **piquant** charm
a. zestful **b.** sarcastic **c.** subtle **d.** bland

20. **decry** our efforts
a. praise **b.** criticize **c.** study **d.** notice

21. the **substantive** candidate
a. substantial **b.** meaningless **c.** noted **d.** public

22. with **unwonted** haste
a. unnecessary **b.** uncommon **c.** customary **d.** reckless

---

VII. Completing the Sentence *From the list of words given below, choose the item that best completes each of the following sentences. Write it in the space given.*

nefarious	**exhume**	**propinquity**
murky	**utopian**	**eulogy**

23. A fellow officer was asked to deliver the ____________________ at the memorial service for the fallen soldier.

24. Archaeologists carefully ____________________ the remains of a warrior who had lain buried for centuries.

25. Divers searched the ____________________ waters for hours before finally recovering the body of the drowning victim.

Name ______________________________

Class ______________ Date ______________ Score ______________

I. Pronunciation *Each of the following words has been divided into syllables. Place the major stress mark (′) after the syllable that is accented when the word is pronounced.*

EXAMPLE: be la bor ⟶ **be la′ bor**

1. de vi ous

2. vis cous

3. cred ence

4. an i mad ver sion

5. em u late

6. con geal

7. pri mor di al

8. in tran si gent

II. Part of Speech *In each of the following groups, circle the item that indicates the part of speech of the word given.*

9. evince
a. noun **b.** adjective **c.** verb **d.** adverb

10. propriety
a. verb **b.** adjective **c.** noun **d.** pronoun

11. largesse
a. adverb **b.** noun **c.** adjective **d.** interjection

12. nefarious
a. verb **b.** noun **c.** preposition **d.** adjective

13. congeal
a. adverb **b.** adjective **c.** verb **d.** conjunction

14. summarily
a. pronoun **b.** verb **c.** adverb **d.** noun

III. Spelling *Circle the word that is incorrectly spelled in each of the following groups. Then supply the correct spelling in the space given.*

15. insendiary overt accost ______________

16. propinquity carping coherant ______________

17. encomium insatiable disemble ______________

18. verdent suppliant tenable ______________

19. celerity ondulate eschew ______________

20. reconnaissance largese avid ______________

IV. Definition *From the lists of words given below, choose the item that corresponds to each of the following definitions. Write it in the space given.*

Group A

cavort	**acquisitive**	**belabor**
maelstrom	**unwonted**	**emulate**

21. not usual or expected; not in character ______________

22. to romp or prance around exuberantly ______________

23. to work on excessively ______________

24. to strive to equal ______________

Group B

talisman	**decry**	**congeal**
gambit	**taciturn**	**piquant**

25. in chess, an opening move that involves the risk of a piece in order to gain a later advantage; any move of this type ______________

26. to condemn, express strong disapproval ______________

27. habitually silent or quiet ______________

28. an object that serves as a charm or is believed to confer magical powers ______________

V. Synonym *In each of the following groups, circle the item that means the same as the* ***boldface*** *word in the introductory phrase.*

29. skillful **temporizing**

a. theorizing **b.** miming **c.** stalling **d.** debating

30. **utopian** views

a. realistic **b.** visionary **c.** old-fashioned **d.** scenic

31. **substantiated** his story

a. filed **b.** validated **c.** concocted **d.** dismissed

32. a **devious** manner

a. blunt **b.** clumsy **c.** shifty **d.** gracious

33. a **myopic** view

a. hazy **b.** farsighted **c.** perceptive **d.** shortsighted

34. a **brackish** flavor
a. tart **b.** sweet **c.** bland **d.** briny

35. wrote a moving **eulogy**
a. testimonial **b.** sermon **c.** account **d.** letter

36. excessive **verbiage**
a. verbosity **b.** coyness **c.** silence **d.** terseness

VI. Antonym *In each of the following groups, circle the item that means the opposite of the **boldface** word in the introductory phrase.*

37. played a **feckless** suitor
a. feeble **b.** romantic **c.** witty **d.** competent

38. **halcyon** weather
a. refreshing **b.** turbulent **c.** seasonable **d.** unchanging

39. the **distraught** witness
a. impartial **b.** agitated **c.** composed **d.** expert

40. **banal** comments
a. original **b.** discrete **c.** trite **d.** sarcastic

41. the **invidious** review
a. malicious **b.** succinct **c.** complimentary **d.** lengthy

42. simply **arrogated** the role
a. loathed **b.** adored **c.** usurped **d.** renounced

43. **exhume** the treasure
a. disinter **b.** bury **c.** discover **d.** divide

44. in the **pejorative** sense
a. favorable **b.** pragmatic **c.** objective **d.** disparaging

VII. Completing the Sentence *From the lists of words given below, choose the item that best completes each of the following sentences. Write it in the space given.*

Group A

encomium	**sacrilege**	**substantive**
myopic	**germane**	**decry**

45. The mayor termed the desecration of the tombstones an intolerable act of ____________ that all decent citizens would deplore.

46. Our favorite sitcom was preempted by a(n) ____________ address by the President, who addressed the nation from the Oval Office.

47. Because we do not have much time to decide the matter, we must discuss only the points that are ____________ to the problem before us.

Group B

reconnaissance	**histrionic**	**evince**
eschew	**verbiage**	**piquant**

48. She has a great voice, but her ____________ abilities leave a lot to be desired.

49. Instead of much-needed action, they have offered us an endless flow of meaningless ____________.

50. Though both of the candidates had pledged to ____________ mudslinging, the campaign soon turned very dirty indeed.

VIII. Framing Sentences (*Optional*) *On the lines provided, write an original sentence that illustrates the meaning and use of each of the following words. Do not merely reproduce one of the sentences given in the text.*

51. belabor

____

____

52. avid

____

____

Name ______________________________

Class ____________ Date ____________ Score ____________

I. Pronunciation *Each of the following words has been divided into syllables. Place the major stress mark (′) after the syllable that is accented when the word is pronounced.*

EXAMPLE: mor dant → **mor′ dant**

1. strat a gem

2. in car ce rate

3. net tle

4. pu sil lan i mous

II. Part of Speech *In each of the following groups, circle the item that indicates the part of speech of the word given.*

5. pecuniary
a. adjective **b.** conjunction **c.** noun **d.** adverb

6. bastion
a. interjection **b.** adjective **c.** adverb **d.** noun

7. glean
a. pronoun **b.** verb **c.** adverb **d.** preposition

III. Spelling *Circle the word that is incorrectly spelled in each of the following groups. Then supply the correct spelling in the space given.*

8. recumbent floatsam jocular ____________

9. ludicrus concord frenetic ____________

10. incumbent atrophy consumate ____________

IV. Definition *From the list of words given below, choose the item that corresponds to each of the following definitions. Write it in the space given.*

glean	**pecuniary**	**pusillanimous**
stratagem	**exigency**	**mordant**

11. contemptibly cowardly or mean spirited ____________

12. urgency; a pressing need; an emergency ____________

13. to gather bit by bit ____________

14. biting or caustic in thought, manner, or style; sharply or bitterly harsh ____________

V. Synonym *In each of the following groups, circle the item that means the same as the **boldface** word in the introductory phrase.*

15. a team in **disarray**
a. defeat **b.** confusion **c.** transition **d.** uniform

16. in a **recumbent** position
a. upright **b.** uncomfortable **c.** dangerous **d.** reclining

17. **incarcerated** the suspect
a. imprisoned **b.** released **c.** followed **d.** questioned

18. a **ludicrous** statement
a. sensational **b.** profound **c.** ridiculous **d.** official

---

VI. Antonym *In each of the following groups, circle the item that means the opposite of the **boldface** word in the introductory phrase.*

19. in a **jocular** mood
a. upbeat **b.** solemn **c.** cheerful **d.** strange

20. an era of **concord**
a. peace **b.** progress **c.** strife **d.** prosperity

21. **groused** about the food
a. complained **b.** inquired **c.** grumbled **d.** raved

22. a **frenetic** pace
a. relaxed **b.** record **c.** temporary **d.** grueling

VII. Completing the Sentence *From the list of words given below, choose the item that best completes each of the following sentences. Write it in the space given.*

atrophy	**jocular**	**grouse**
bastion	**incumbent**	**pusillanimous**

23. The harshest critics characterized the government's willingness to give in to the dictator's demands as nothing less than ____________________ appeasement.

24. The patient was confined to a hospital bed for so long that the muscles in her legs began to ____________________.

25. It is a general rule of politics that a(n) ____________________ running for reelection has a decided advantage over the challenger.

Name ______________________________

Class ______________ Date ______________ Score ______________

I. Pronunciation *Each of the following words has been divided into syllables. Place the major stress mark (′) after the syllable that is accented when the word is pronounced.*

EXAMPLE: de lin e ate → **de lin′ e ate**

1. id i o syn cra sy

2. u biq ui tous

3. de praved

4. fig ment

II. Part of Speech *In each of the following groups, circle the item that indicates the part of speech of the word given.*

5. delineate
a. adjective **b.** adverb **c.** noun **d.** verb

6. sophistry
a. pronoun **b.** noun **c.** adverb **d.** verb

7. fecund
a. noun **b.** verb **c.** adjective **d.** conjunction

III. Spelling *Circle the word that is incorrectly spelled in each of the following groups. Then supply the correct spelling in the space given.*

8. sumptuous esoteric ignomeny ______________

9. nuance enarvate fiat ______________

10. garner mundane halow ______________

IV. Definition *From the list of words given below, choose the item that corresponds to each of the following definitions. Write it in the space given.*

overweening **figment** **acuity**
penchant **reputed** **idiosyncrasy**

11. according to general belief; alleged ______________

12. conceited, presumptuous; excessive ______________

13. sharpness (particularly of the mind or senses) ______________

14. a strong attraction or inclination ______________

V. Synonym *In each of the following groups, circle the item that means the same as the **boldface** word in the introductory phrase.*

15. issued a **fiat**
a. decree **b.** warning **c.** description **d.** request

16. **ubiquitous** graffiti
a. clever **b.** obscene **c.** pervasive **d.** ancient

17. **delineate** our duties
a. describe **b.** neglect **c.** perform **d.** protest

18. fooled by his **sophistry**
a. reputation **b.** casuistry **c.** politeness **d.** intentions

---

VI. Antonym *In each of the following groups, circle the item that means the opposite of the **boldface** word in the introductory phrase.*

19. **esoteric** references
a. cryptic **b.** scholarly **c.** intelligible **d.** recondite

20. **mundane** concerns
a. foolish **b.** financial **c.** ordinary **d.** transcendental

21. **enervated** by the experience
a. strengthened **b.** saddened **c.** exhausted **d.** confused

22. **sumptuous** accommodations
a. luxurious **b.** spartan **c.** recent **d.** strange

VII. Completing the Sentence *From the list of words given below, choose the item that best completes each of the following sentences. Write it in the space given.*

nuance	**penchant**	**garner**
reputed	**depraved**	**enervate**

23. It takes years of study to understand the subtle ____________ of meaning in a foreign language.

24. The movie earned millions at the box office and ____________ five Academy Awards to boot.

25. Only a truly ____________ mind could have conceived such an evil and perverted scheme.

Name ______________________________

Class ______________ Date ______________ Score ______________

I. Pronunciation *Each of the following words has been divided into syllables. Place the major stress mark (′) after the syllable that is accented when the word is pronounced.*

EXAMPLE: com plic i ty → **comp plic′ i ty**

1. trav e sty

2. der e lict

3. mo tif

4. in ter mit tent

II. Part of Speech *In each of the following groups, circle the item that indicates the part of speech of the word given.*

5. equity
a. verb **b.** adjective **c.** noun **d.** preposition

6. indubitable
a. noun **b.** verb **c.** adverb **d.** adjective

7. plenary
a. adjective **b.** noun **c.** verb **d.** conjunction

III. Spelling *Circle the word that is incorrectly spelled in each of the following groups. Then supply the correct spelling in the space given.*

8. diatribe noephyte moot ______________

9. efigy indictment sylvan ______________

10. inane perspicasity surveillance ______________

IV. Definition *From the list of words given below, choose the item that corresponds to each of the following definitions. Write it in the space given.*

travesty **testy** **plenary**
abject **agnostic** **complicity**

11. involvement in wrongdoing ______________

12. wretched; base; complete and unrelieved ______________

13. a grotesque or grossly inferior representation ______________

14. one who believes that nothing is known about God; a skeptic ______________

V. Synonym *In each of the following groups, circle the item that means the same as the* ***boldface*** *word in the introductory phrase.*

15. a **moot** issue
a. unresolved **b.** pressing **c.** secondary **d.** social

16. delivered a **diatribe**
a. baby **b.** harangue **c.** newspaper **d.** package

17. **plenary** powers
a. restricted **b.** hereditary **c.** supernatural **d.** unlimited

18. a **sylvan** setting
a. urban **b.** colonial **c.** barren **d.** forested

VI. Antonym *In each of the following groups, circle the item that means the opposite of the* ***boldface*** *word in the introductory phrase.*

19. classed with the **neophytes**
a. novices **b.** vertebrates **c.** minerals **d.** experts

20. a **testy** waiter
a. imperturbable **b.** irritable **c.** inexperienced **d.** exasperated

21. **indubitable** honesty
a. indisputable **b.** doubtful **c.** exemplary **d.** unquestionable

22. **inane** comments
a. fatuous **b.** brief **c.** sensible **d.** recent

VII. Completing the Sentence *From the list of words given below, choose the item that best completes each of the following sentences. Write it in the space given.*

abject	**indictment**	**motif**
surveillance	**intermittent**	**moot**

23. The grand jury handed down felony ____________________ against several of the officials involved in the scandal.

24. Although the weather forecast had called for steady rain, all we got were ____________________ showers.

25. Police kept the suspect under close ____________________ in the hope that he would lead them to the gang's hideout.

Name ______________________________

Class ____________ Date ____________ Score ____________

I. Pronunciation *Each of the following words has been divided into syllables. Place the major stress mark (′) after the syllable that is accented when the word is pronounced.*

EXAMPLE: ag nos tic ⟶ **ag nos′ tic**

1. my op ic

2. con geal

3. in du bi ta ble

4. ig no min y

5. per spi cac it y

6. fre net ic

7. em u late

8. fec und

II. Part of Speech *In each of the following groups, circle the item that indicates the part of speech of the word given.*

9. invidious
a. verb **b.** adjective **c.** conjunction **d.** pronoun

10. accost
a. verb **b.** conjunction **c.** adjective **d.** noun

11. nuance
a. adverb **b.** adjective **c.** noun **d.** interjection

12. abject
a. noun **b.** preposition **c.** adjective **d.** adverb

13. propinquity
a. noun **b.** preposition **c.** adjective **d.** interjection

14. glean
a. adjective **b.** pronoun **c.** noun **d.** verb

III. Spelling *Circle the word that is incorrectly spelled in each of the following groups. Then supply the correct spelling in the space given.*

15. intermittent plenary gleen ____________

16. sophistry evinse eschew ____________

17. inditement depraved grouse ____________

18. incumbent substantive ennervate ____________

19. histrionic dissaray figment ____________

20. enconium indubitable pecuniary ____________

IV. Definition *From the lists of words given below, choose the item that corresponds to each of the following definitions. Write it in the space given.*

Group A

halcyon	**garner**	**overweening**
feckless	**equity**	**sacrilege**

21. to acquire as the result of effort; to gather and store away ________________

22. presumptuous or excessive ________________

23. the state of being just or impartial; fair and equal treatment ________________

24. peaceful; happy, golden, prosperous ________________

Group B

fiat	**emulate**	**exhume**
flotsam	**germane**	**sylvan**

25. to remove from a grave; to bring to light, unearth ________________

26. an arbitrary order or decree ________________

27. relevant, appropriate, apropos ________________

28. characteristic of forests; living or located in a forest; wooded ________________

V. Synonym *In each of the following groups, circle the item that means the same as the* ***boldface*** *word in the introductory phrase.*

29. a **coherent** plan of action

a. meaningful **b.** secret **c.** novel **d.** complicated

30. **inane** remarks

a. sarcastic **b.** lengthy **c.** insightful **d.** vapid

31. a **bastion** of propriety

a. criterion **b.** sense **c.** stronghold **d.** proponent

32. **mordant** observations

a. sympathetic **b.** brilliant **c.** insightful **d.** acrimonious

33. a collection of **talismans**

a. rare books **b.** amulets **c.** curios **d.** paintings

34. **esoteric** doctrines
a. traditional b. cryptic c. controversial d. orthodox

35. an unpleasantly **viscous** consistency
a. gelatinous b. grainy c. airy d. watery

36. watched the calves **cavort**
a. gambol b. eat c. sleep d. race

VI. Antonym *In each of the following groups, circle the item that means the opposite of the **boldface** word in the introductory phrase.*

37. a **sumptuous** holiday meal
a. spartan b. lavish c. low-calorie d. colorful

38. found the issue **moot**
a. undebatable b. academic c. obvious d. settled

39. preferred to be **recumbent**
a. supine b. inside c. upright d. outside

40. the patron's **largesse**
a. generosity b. stinginess c. reputation d. demands

41. **ubiquitous** rumors
a. pervasive b. rare c. groundless d. scandalous

42. **murky** depths
a. cloudy b. bottomless c. limpid d. unexplored

43. named as the **incendiary**
a. arsonist b. loser c. winner d. peacemaker

44. **pusillanimous** conduct
a. inexcusable b. craven c. proper d. daring

VII. Completing the Sentence *From the lists of words given below, choose the item that best completes each of the following sentences. Write it in the space given.*

Group A

undulate	**penchant**	**nefarious**
taciturn	**diatribe**	**incarcerate**

45. President Coolidge's ______________ disposition earned him the nickname "Silent Cal."

46. Although he has spent most of his life in the business world, he shows a distinct ______________ for the arts.

47. During World War II, hundreds of Americans were ______________ in detention camps simply because of their Japanese ancestry.

Group B

consummate	**idiosyncrasy**	**arrogate**
distraught	**gambit**	**delineate**

48. The map that the teacher drew for the children ______________ all of the major buildings and landmarks of their community.

49. We had great respect for our chemistry professor, but we found her ______________ both odd and curiously unsettling.

50. The great victory was largely due to the daring ______________ that had so confused the enemy at the outset of the battle.

VIII. Framing Sentences (*Optional*) *On the lines provided, write an original sentence that illustrates the meaning and use of each of the following words. Do not merely reproduce one of the sentences given in the text.*

51. complicity

____

____

52. ludicrous

____

____

Name ______________________________

Class ______________ Date ______________ Score ______________

I. Pronunciation *Each of the following words has been divided into syllables. Place the major stress mark (′) after the syllable that is accented when the word is pronounced.*

EXAMPLE: rai ment ⟶ **rai′ ment**

1. per ti na cious

2. pic a yune

3. fe lic i tous

4. con viv i al

II. Part of Speech *In each of the following groups, circle the item that indicates the part of speech of the word given.*

5. bestial
a. verb **b.** noun **c.** adjective **d.** interjection

6. effrontery
a. adverb **b.** adjective **c.** conjunction **d.** noun

7. allay
a. noun **b.** verb **c.** preposition **d.** adjective

III. Spelling *Circle the word that is incorrectly spelled in each of the following groups. Then supply the correct spelling in the space given.*

8. illusury counterpart garish ______________

9. embelish furtive ephemeral ______________

10. jettison coteree inordinate ______________

IV. Definition *From the list of words given below, choose the item that corresponds to each of the following definitions. Write it in the space given.*

effrontery **misanthrope** **indigent**
convivial **pertinacious** **demur**

11. one who hates or despises people ______________

12. shameless boldness, impudence ______________

13. very persistent; holding firmly to a course of action; refusing to be put off or denied ______________

14. to object or take exception to ______________

V. Synonym *In each of the following groups, circle the item that means the same as the **boldface** word in the introductory phrase.*

15. inordinate demands

a. modest **b.** excessive **c.** curious **d.** new

16. costly **raiment**

a. repairs **b.** mistakes **c.** attire **d.** programs

17. picayune criticisms

a. scholarly **b.** perceptive **c.** forceful **d.** trifling

18. a **furtive** manner

a. sneaky **b.** direct **c.** pleasing **d.** candid

VI. Antonym *In each of the following groups, circle the item that means the opposite of the **boldface** word in the introductory phrase.*

19. an **ephemeral** success

a. enduring **b.** short-lived **c.** phenomenal **d.** enviable

20. allay their anxiety

a. intensify **b.** justify **c.** ridicule **d.** alleviate

21. a **convivial** group

a. genial **b.** unsociable **c.** festive **d.** merry

22. garish costumes

a. gaudy **b.** traditional **c.** rented **d.** understated

VII. Completing the Sentence *From the list of words given below, choose the item that best completes each of the following sentences. Write it in the space given.*

felicitous	**jettison**	**coterie**
indigent	**bestial**	**counterpart**

23. In preparation for the emergency landing, the pilot ____________________ the jet's extra fuel as well as the cargo on board.

24. The food and clothing collected in the charity drive were distributed to ____________________ families in the community.

25. The director of the agency met with her ____________________ from other governmental departments to coordinate administration policy.

Name ______________________________

Class ______________ Date ______________ Score ______________

I. Pronunciation *Each of the following words has been divided into syllables. Place the major stress mark (′) after the syllable that is accented when the word is pronounced.*

EXAMPLE: bad i nage ⟶ **bad i nage′**

1. sat u rate

2. lack a dai si cal

3. al lege

4. re cant

II. Part of Speech *In each of the following groups, circle the item that indicates the part of speech of the word given.*

5. paucity
a. adjective **b.** verb **c.** noun **d.** interjection

6. portend
a. adverb **b.** noun **c.** preposition **d.** verb

7. macabre
a. adjective **b.** adverb **c.** verb **d.** noun

III. Spelling *Circle the word that is incorrectly spelled in each of the following groups. Then supply the correct spelling in the space given.*

8. fatuous liteny countermand ______________

9. exacerbate raze juggernaught ______________

10. consiliate echelon irrefutable ______________

IV. Definition *From the list of words given below, choose the item that corresponds to each of the following definitions. Write it in the space given.*

saturate **arrant** **portend**
saturnine **macabre** **slough**

11. thoroughgoing; shameless, blatant ______________

12. to cast off, discard ______________

13. to give advance warning of ______________

14. of gloomy or surly disposition ______________

V. Synonym *In each of the following groups, circle the item that means the same as the **boldface** word in the introductory phrase.*

15. **recant** her testimony
   a. corroborate   b. record   c. read back   d. retract

16. amused by their **badinage**
   a. excuses   b. banter   c. appearance   d. singing

17. **countermand** a directive
   a. revoke   b. issue   c. clarify   d. ignore

18. **irrefutable** evidence
   a. tainted   b. circumstantial   c. indisputable   d. dubious

---

VI. Antonym *In each of the following groups, circle the item that means the opposite of the **boldface** word in the introductory phrase.*

19. a **paucity** of resources
   a. abundance   b. scarcity   c. use   d. waste

20. a **fatuous** comment
   a. perceptive   b. foolish   c. brief   d. recent

21. a **saturnine** disposition
   a. grim   b. surly   c. ugly   d. cheerful

22. **exacerbate** the problem
   a. aggravate   b. alleviate   c. ignore   d. discuss

VII. Completing the Sentence *From the list of words given below, choose the item that best completes each of the following sentences. Write it in the space given.*

allege	**lackadaisical**	**portend**
raze	**irrefutable**	**echelon**

23. Hundreds gathered to protest the developer's plan to ________________ the historic theater to make room for a high-rise office building.

24. The coach gave our entire team a chewing out for our halfhearted and ________________ play in our last game.

25. News concerning the sensitive negotiations was circulated only among members of the highest ________________ of government.

Name ____________________

Class __________ Date __________ Score __________

I. Pronunciation *Each of the following words has been divided into syllables. Place the major stress mark (′) after the syllable that is accented when the word is pronounced.*

EXAMPLE: ca lum ni ate → **ca lum′ ni ate**

1. col lu sion

2. man date

3. red o lent

4. ac cla ma tion

II. Part of Speech *In each of the following groups, circle the item that indicates the part of speech of the word given.*

5. redolent
a. verb **b.** preposition **c.** adjective **d.** noun

6. paroxysm
a. noun **b.** conjunction **c.** adjective **d.** verb

7. calumniate
a. adjective **b.** noun **c.** verb **d.** adverb

III. Spelling *Circle the word that is incorrectly spelled in each of the following groups. Then supply the correct spelling in the space given.*

8. increment paltry unremitting __________

9. tyro vaccilate peregrination __________

10. refulgent imperturbable buccolic __________

IV. Definition *From the list of words given below, choose the item that corresponds to each of the following definitions. Write it in the space given.*

chary **mandate** **dilettante**
paroxysm **vituperative** **shibboleth**

11. extremely cautious, hesitant __________

12. harshly abusive __________

13. a dabbler in the arts __________

14. a word or expression that distinguishes a particular group of people __________

V. Synonym *In each of the following groups, circle the item that means the same as the **boldface** word in the introductory phrase.*

15. a **paltry** amount

a. exact **b.** piddling **c.** incorrect **d.** substantial

16. accused them of **pedantry**

a. hairsplitting **b.** treason **c.** malingering **d.** cowardice

17. **vituperative** remarks

a. complimentary **b.** brief **c.** flattering **d.** abusive

18. a record of their **peregrinations**

a. dreams **b.** expenses **c.** travels **d.** victories

VI. Antonym *In each of the following groups, circle the item that means the opposite of the **boldface** word in the introductory phrase.*

19. **unremitting** efforts

a. desultory **b.** tireless **c.** recent **d.** successful

20. an **imperturbable** manager

a. unflappable **b.** experienced **c.** excitable **d.** skillful

21. a **bucolic** setting

a. rural **b.** stage **c.** neglected **d.** urban

22. performed like a **tyro**

a. child **b.** rookie **c.** coward **d.** veteran

VII. Completing the Sentence *From the list of words given below, choose the item that best completes each of the following sentences. Write it in the space given.*

dilettante	**acclamation**	**vacillate**
vituperative	**calumniate**	**refulgent**

23. We could see the ____________________ face of the moon reflected on the sea's tranquil surface.

24. The measure, which enjoyed bipartisan support in Congress, was passed by ____________________ in both houses.

25. There seems no point to the vicious smears contained in the book other than to ____________________ the memory of a great leader.

Name ______________________________

Class ______________ Date ______________ Score ______________

I. Pronunciation *Each of the following words has been divided into syllables. Place the major stress mark (ʹ) after the syllable that is accented when the word is pronounced.*

EXAMPLE: gam bit ⟶ **gamʹ bit**

1. de cry

2. pen chant

3. mis an thrope

4. im per tur ba ble

5. in di gent

6. sub stan ti ate

7. fat u ous

8. par ox ysm

II. Part of Speech *In each of the following groups, circle the item that indicates the part of speech of the word given.*

9. motif
a. preposition **b.** verb **c.** noun **d.** pronoun

10. embellish
a. noun **b.** adverb **c.** preposition **d.** verb

11. incarcerate
a. adverb **b.** conjunction **c.** pronoun **d.** verb

12. peregrination
a. interjection **b.** noun **c.** verb **d.** pronoun

13. saturnine
a. adverb **b.** adjective **c.** verb **d.** conjunction

14. mundane
a. adjective **b.** verb **c.** interjection **d.** noun

III. Spelling *Circle the word that is incorrectly spelled in each of the following groups. Then supply the correct spelling in the space given.*

15. germane pedentry myopic ______________

16. inordinite fiat portend ______________

17. agnostic echelon equaty ______________

18. irrefutible credence stratagem ______________

19. demur sofestry feckless ______________

20. ludicrous temporize exegeansy ______________

IV. Definition *From the lists of words given below, choose the item that corresponds to each of the following definitions. Write it in the space given.*

Group A

mandate	**tenable**	**fatuous**
allay	**perspicacity**	**exhume**

21. stupid or foolish in a self-satisfied way ________________

22. an authoritative command, formal order, or authorization; to issue such an order ________________

23. to calm or pacify; to soothe; to lessen or relieve ________________

24. keenness of observing and understanding ________________

Group B

fecund	**nettle**	**intransigent**
maelstrom	**moot**	**substantive**

25. refusing to compromise, irreconcilable ________________

26. a whirlpool of great size and violence; any situation resembling such a whirlpool ________________

27. to vex or irritate severely ________________

28. real, having a solid basis ________________

V. Synonym *In each of the following groups, circle the item that means the same as the **boldface** word in the introductory phrase.*

29. surprised by their **celerity**
a. alacrity **b.** generosity **c.** cowardice **d.** reputation

30. **emulate** the actress
a. praise **b.** mimic **c.** direct **d.** criticize

31. **jettison** the cargo
a. store **b.** ship **c.** tax **d.** discard

32. **exacerbate** the injury
a. treat **b.** report **c.** intensify **d.** prevent

33. known for their **idiosyncrasies**
a. jokes **b.** intelligence **c.** wealth **d.** eccentricities

34. a **frenetic** atmosphere
a. sinister **b.** peaceful **c.** congenial **d.** frenzied

35. **allege** the facts
a. assert **b.** answer **c.** allay **d.** atrophy

36. warmed by the **acclamation**
a. recognition **b.** generosity **c.** ovation **d.** kindness

---

VI. Antonym *In each of the following groups, circle the item that means the opposite of the **boldface** word in the introductory phrase.*

37. a decidedly **mordant** sense of humor
a. mild **b.** caustic **c.** zany **d.** unique

38. **bestial** treatment
a. brutal **b.** silent **c.** clement **d.** efficient

39. printed the **eulogy**
a. philippic **b.** interview **c.** sermon **d.** tribute

40. **intermittent** snow
a. sporadic **b.** light **c.** drifting **d.** uninterrupted

41. a **lackadaisical** performance
a. indifferent **b.** energetic **c.** unrehearsed **d.** postponed

42. a **brackish** solution
a. natural **b.** clear **c.** muddy **d.** patented

43. **conciliate** an old foe
a. identify **b.** remember **c.** alienate **d.** appease

44. a **bucolic** theme
a. pastoral **b.** cryptic **c.** traditional **d.** metropolitan

VII. Completing the Sentence *From the lists of words given below, choose the item that best completes each of the following sentences. Write it in the space given.*

Group A

paucity	**juggernaut**	**ephemeral**
eschew	**pejorative**	**redolent**

45. The candidate's campaign manager launched a(n) ________________ of incessant radio and TV advertising spots that were impossible to ignore.

46. A recently published report concluded that the ________________ of natural resources would make the area unattractive to developers.

47. During the anarchy of the fourth century, one ________________ Roman emperor followed another in quick succession.

Group B

furtive	**acuity**	**derelict**
consummate	**badinage**	**vacillate**

48. Not long after its owner abandoned it, the ________________ car was towed to the junk yard.

49. Though there are still a few minor details to iron out, we expect to ________________ the deal sometime this week.

50. Some birds have such remarkable ________________ of vision that they can spot small prey from hundreds of feet in the air.

VIII. Framing Sentences (*Optional*) *On the lines provided, write an original sentence that illustrates the meaning and use of each of the following words. Do not merely reproduce one of the sentences given in the text.*

51. allege

____

____

52. collusion

____

____

Name ______________________________

Class ____________ Date ____________ Score ____________

I. Pronunciation *Each of the following words has been divided into syllables. Place the major stress mark (′) after the syllable that is accented when the word is pronounced.*

EXAMPLE: lu mi nous ⟶ **lu′ mi nous**

1. cav il

2. pe remp to ry

3. re con noit er

4. in ure

II. Part of Speech *In each of the following groups, circle the item that indicates the part of speech of the word given.*

5. foible
a. conjunction **b.** adverb **c.** adjective **d.** noun

6. forgo
a. adjective **b.** preposition **c.** verb **d.** noun

7. askance
a. noun **b.** verb **c.** interjection **d.** adverb

III. Spelling *Circle the word that is incorrectly spelled in each of the following groups. Then supply the correct spelling in the space given.*

8. sporadic rebuff atenuate ____________

9. penitant decimate obtuse ____________

10. obsequious shambels charlatan ____________

IV. Definition *From the list of words given below, choose the item that corresponds to each of the following definitions. Write it in the space given.*

askance	**cavil**	**oscillate**
inure	**benign**	**peremptory**

11. to swing back and forth; to fluctuate ____________

12. to toughen, harden; to render used to something by exposure ____________

13. having the nature of a command ____________

14. with suspicion, mistrust, or disapproval ____________

V. Synonym *In each of the following groups, circle the item that means the same as the **boldface** word in the introductory phrase.*

15. a **luminous** body
 a. thin b. massive c. shadowy d. radiant

16. an **obtuse** comment
 a. alert b. dull-witted c. gloomy d. cheerful

17. a **peremptory** tone of voice
 a. mild b. ghostly c. sarcastic d. commanding

18. called him a **charlatan**
 a. miser b. hero c. fraud d. genius

VI. Antonym *In each of the following groups, circle the item that means the opposite of the **boldface** word in the introductory phrase.*

19. **rebuff** the offer
 a. spurn b. accept c. devise d. criticize

20. **benign** effects
 a. deleterious b. salutary c. unexpected d. minimal

21. an **obsequious** manner
 a. servile b. disgusting c. strange d. overbearing

22. **sporadic** gunfire
 a. deadly b. distant c. steady d. intermittent

VII. Completing the Sentence *From the list of words given below, choose the item that best completes each of the following sentences. Write it in the space given.*

fraught	**foible**	**obtuse**
forgo	**decimate**	**charlatan**

23. Instead of dwelling on the candidate's ________________, why don't you consider her many strong points?

24. Enemy machine-gun fire ________________ the dense columns of infantry advancing across the open field.

25. The volunteers undertook the rescue mission knowing full well that it was ________________ with peril.

Name ______________________________

Class ______________ Date ______________ Score ______________

I. Pronunciation *Each of the following words has been divided into syllables. Place the major stress mark (′) after the syllable that is accented when the word is pronounced.*

EXAMPLE: am bi ent ⟶ **am′ bi ent**

1. mor i bund
2. ca bal
3. a sper i ty
4. in ex or a ble

II. Part of Speech *In each of the following groups, circle the item that indicates the part of speech of the word given.*

5. necromancer
   a. adjective **b.** noun **c.** verb **d.** preposition
6. deprecate
   a. verb **b.** adjective **c.** noun **d.** conjunction
7. rife
   a. pronoun **b.** adjective **c.** interjection **d.** adverb

III. Spelling *Circle the word that is incorrectly spelled in each of the following groups. Then supply the correct spelling in the space given.*

8. delectable eklectic winnow ______________
9. onerous impecunious flassid ______________
10. secquester rudiments abrogate ______________

IV. Definition *From the list of words given below, choose the item that corresponds to each of the following definitions. Write it in the space given.*

burnish	**moribund**	**ambient**
ebullient	**rife**	**detritus**

11. completely surrounding ______________
12. dying, on the way out ______________
13. to polish; to gloss, luster ______________
14. loose bits and pieces of material resulting from disintegration or wearing away ______________

V. Synonym *In each of the following groups, circle the item that means the same as the **boldface** word in the introductory phrase.*

15. part of the **cabal**
a. conspiracy **b.** message **c.** solution **d.** mechanism

16. an **impecunious** youth
a. reckless **b.** penniless **c.** anonymous **d.** uneducated

17. the skills of a **necromancer**
a. athlete **b.** mechanic **c.** magician **d.** executive

18. a **delectable** dish
a. broken **b.** boring **c.** traditional **d.** delicious

VI. Antonym *In each of the following groups, circle the item that means the opposite of the **boldface** word in the introductory phrase.*

19. surprised by the **asperity** of their remarks
a. stupidity **b.** uncertainty **c.** mildness **d.** harshness

20. **deprecate** our achievements
a. praise **b.** belittle **c.** study **d.** describe

21. **abrogate** the agreement
a. cancel **b.** break **c.** ratify **d.** criticize

22. an **ebullient** crowd
a. huge **b.** sullen **c.** exuberant **d.** perceptive

VII. Completing the Sentence *From the list of words given below, choose the item that best completes each of the following sentences. Write it in the space given.*

burnish	**inexorable**	**winnow**
onerous	**rudiments**	**eclectic**

23. He has fallen into the habit of doing only the easy chores and leaving all of the ________________ tasks to others.

24. My mother spent hours polishing and ________________ the antique brass bowl she found in the antique shop.

25. In our introductory Spanish course, we were taught basic vocabulary and the ________________ of grammar.

Name ______________________________

Class ______________ Date ______________ Score ______________

I. Pronunciation *Each of the following words has been divided into syllables. Place the major stress mark (′) after the syllable that is accented when the word is pronounced.*

EXAMPLE: la con ic ⟶ **la con′ ic**

1. gre gar i ous

2. de funct

3. tan ta mount

4. om ni pre sent

II. Part of Speech *In each of the following groups, circle the item that indicates the part of speech of the word given.*

5. omnipresent
a. adverb **b.** noun **c.** conjunction **d.** adjective

6. requite
a. noun **b.** verb **c.** adverb **d.** preposition

7. nadir
a. adjective **b.** pronoun **c.** noun **d.** verb

III. Spelling *Circle the word that is incorrectly spelled in each of the following groups. Then supply the correct spelling in the space given.*

8. perfunctory languish mendascious ______________

9. asthetic espouse irreparable ______________

10. hapless fettish impeccable ______________

IV. Definition *From the list of words given below, choose the item that corresponds to each of the following definitions. Write it in the space given.*

plaintive	**tantamount**	**interpolate**
discomfit	**importune**	**defunct**

11. to insert between other parts or things ______________

12. to trouble with demands; to beg ______________

13. equivalent, having the same meaning, value, or effect ______________

14. no longer existing or functioning, dead ______________

V. Synonym *In each of the following groups, circle the item that means the same as the **boldface** word in the introductory phrase.*

15. **impeccable** manners
   a. coarse **b.** foreign **c.** faulty **d.** flawless
16. **discomfit** our opponents
   a. appease **b.** thwart **c.** fear **d.** surrender to
17. a **perfunctory** examination
   a. superficial **b.** painstaking **c.** professional **d.** recent
18. a **plaintive** note
   a. happy **b.** uncertain **c.** melancholy **d.** hopeful

---

VI. Antonym *In each of the following groups, circle the item that means the opposite of the **boldface** word in the introductory phrase.*

19. **laconic** remarks
   a. verbose **b.** analytical **c.** critical **d.** terse
20. a **gregarious** neighbor
   a. noisy **b.** sociable **c.** reclusive **d.** helpful
21. a **hapless** youth
   a. unlucky **b.** clumsy **c.** easygoing **d.** fortunate
22. **espoused** our cause
   a. supported **b.** repudiated **c.** hailed **d.** embraced

---

VII. Completing the Sentence *From the list of words given below, choose the item that best completes each of the following sentences. Write it in the space given.*

impeccable	**omnipresent**	**requite**
languish	**tantamount**	**irreparable**

23. My worst fears were confirmed when the mechanic told me that the damage to my bike was ____________.
24. The judge's forceful request to hand over the pertinent documents immediately was delivered in such a way as to be ____________ to a court order.
25. The provisional government freed the scores of political prisoners who had ____________ in the old regime's detention centers.

Name ____________________

Class ____________ Date ____________ Score ____________

I. Pronunciation *Each of the following words has been divided into syllables. Place the major stress mark (′) after the syllable that is accented when the word is pronounced.*

EXAMPLE: re buff ⟶ **re buff′**

1. a tro phy

2. ca vort

3. de mur

4. in ter po late

5. soph i stry

6. jug ger naut

7. en co mi um

8. un re mit ting

9. mael strom

10. spo rad ic

11. sur veil lance

12. im pe cu ni ous

II. Part of Speech *In each of the following groups, circle the item that indicates the part of speech of the word given.*

13. detritus
a. conjunction **b.** adjective **c.** pronoun **d.** noun

14. overweening
a. noun **b.** adjective **c.** conjunction **d.** adverb

15. pertinacious
a. adverb **b.** conjunction **c.** noun **d.** adjective

16. litany
a. verb **b.** adverb **c.** noun **d.** preposition

17. indictment
a. conjunction **b.** noun **c.** verb **d.** adverb

18. arrogate
a. verb **b.** interjection **c.** noun **d.** adjective

19. espouse
a. preposition **b.** verb **c.** interjection **d.** noun

20. jocular
a. adjective **b.** noun **c.** adverb **d.** pronoun

21. conciliate
a. verb **b.** noun **c.** preposition **d.** adjective

III. Spelling *Circle the word that is incorrectly spelled in each of the following groups. Then supply the correct spelling in the space given.*

22. lackonic allay calumniate ____________

23. discomfit sumtuous badinage ____________

24. banal alledge ubiquitous ____________

25. colusion testy slough ____________

26. derelict bernish bastion ____________

27. complisity picayune nadir ____________

28. forgo fraut brackish ____________

29. tyro delectable murkey ____________

30. reconnoiter verbiage fertive ____________

IV. Definition *From the lists of words given below, choose the item that corresponds to each of the following definitions. Write it in the space given.*

Group A

requite	**exacerbate**	**viscous**
inexorable	**vacillate**	**effigy**

31. having a gelatinous or gluey quality; lacking in easy movement ____________

32. to make suitable repayment; to make retaliation; to reciprocate ____________

33. a crude image of a despised person ____________

34. to swing indecisively from one idea or course of action to another ____________

Group B

coterie	**winnow**	**askance**
saturnine	**accost**	**ignominy**

35. to approach and speak to first ____________

36. of gloomy or surly disposition; cold or sluggish in mood ____________

37. to get rid of something unwanted; to sift through to obtain what is desirable ____________

38. public shame and disgrace ____________

Group C

pusillanimous	**eschew**	**impeccable**
counterpart	**acclamation**	**cavil**

39. a person or thing closely resembling or corresponding to another ________________

40. to find fault in a petty way, carp; a trivial objection or criticism ________________

41. to avoid, shun, keep away from, steer clear of ________________

42. contemptibly cowardly or mean-spirited ________________

V. Synonym *In each of the following groups, circle the item that means the same as the **boldface** word in the introductory phrase.*

43. the **piquant** odor
a. sweet **b.** pungent **c.** offensive **d.** mild

44. a **flaccid** handshake
a. firm **b.** limp **c.** secret **d.** polite

45. a **tenable** argument
a. convoluted **b.** surprising **c.** nonsensical **d.** maintainable

46. **gregarious** species
a. sociable **b.** endangered **c.** extinct **d.** related

47. **onerous** tasks
a. monotonous **b.** oppressive **c.** challenging **d.** simple

48. **interpolate** the answers
a. intercept **b.** interpose **c.** interview **d.** interrupt

49. **avid** bowlers
a. professional **b.** novice **c.** keen **d.** accomplished

50. the **obsequious** salesperson
a. overbearing **b.** experienced **c.** mealy-mouthed **d.** helpful

51. **rebuff** their suggestion
a. reject **b.** welcome **c.** expand **d.** vote on

52. **pecuniary** matters
a. judicial **b.** financial **c.** legislative **d.** academic

53. repeated the **motif**
a. warning **b.** order **c.** question **d.** theme

54. **razed** the old pier
a. rebuilt **b.** explored **c.** tore down **d.** berthed

VI. Antonym *In each of the following groups, circle the item that means the opposite of the* ***boldface*** *word in the introductory phrase.*

55. **hallowed** ground
a. blessed **b.** eroded **c.** tilled **d.** defiled

56. **countermand** the sentence
a. revoke **b.** protest **c.** negotiate **d.** reassert

57. a **peremptory** dismissal
a. premature **b.** sudden **c.** tentative **d.** curt

58. forgave their **foibles**
a. virtues **b.** weaknesses **c.** misdeeds **d.** insults

59. **incarcerated** the animals
a. maltreated **b.** liberated **c.** trained **d.** caged

60. a **perfunctory** examination
a. mandatory **b.** superficial **c.** recent **d.** thorough

61. **flaccid** physique
a. soft **b.** firm **c.** impressive **d.** nondescript

62. **forgo** a vacation
a. refrain from **b.** add on to **c.** indulge in **d.** return from

63. **illusory** problems
a. fictitious **b.** unsolvable **c.** real **d.** complex

64. decidedly **vituperative** in tone
a. laudatory **b.** conspiratorial **c.** insulting **d.** negative

65. **substantiated** the rumors
a. circulated **b.** disproved **c.** confirmed **d.** ignored

66. a **utopian** community
a. realistic **b.** close-knit **c.** suburban **d.** visionary

VII. Completing the Sentence *From the lists of words given below, choose the item that best completes each of the following sentences. Write it in the space given.*

Group A

felicitous	**emulate**	**cabal**
macabre	**paroxysm**	**temporize**

67. An effective leader does not ____________________ in a crisis but acts swiftly and decisively to resolve the situation.

68. One of the king's secret agents infiltrated the ____________________ of disaffected officers who were conspiring to overthrow the regime.

69. Though she was unexpectedly called on to speak, the remarks she made were both appropriate and ____________________.

Group B

fetish	**oscillate**	**glean**
litany	**benign**	**garish**

70. Much of the news about the economy has been discouraging, but we hope to ____________________ a few shreds of comfort from the latest reports.

71. Angry union leaders recited a whole ____________________ of grievances that management had yet to address.

72. Needless to say, my uncle was most relieved when laboratory tests showed the growth on his back to be ____________________.

Group C

ebullient	**mandate**	**charlatan**
importune	**reputed**	**congeal**

73. He is ____________________ to be a top-notch tennis player, but I am confident that I can hold my own against him on the court.

74. The streets of the bazaar were lined with scores of ragged beggars, who ____________________ passing tourists for handouts.

75. In view of his narrow margin of victory at the polls, it seemed somewhat presumptuous for the new mayor-elect to claim he had received a clear ____________________ from the voters.

VIII. Framing Sentences (*Optional*)

On the lines provided, write an original sentence that illustrates the meaning and use of each of the following words. Do not merely reproduce one of the sentences given in the text.

76. effrontery

77. grouse

78. inure

79. tantamount

80. eclectic

Name ____________

Class ____________ Date ____________ Score ____________

I. Pronunciation *Each of the following words has been divided into syllables. Place the major stress mark (′) after the syllable that is accented when the word is pronounced.*

EXAMPLE: cog ni zant ⟶ **cog′ ni zant**

1. mach i na tion

2. pu ta tive

3. op pro bri um

4. ef fi ca cy

II. Part of Speech *In each of the following groups, circle the item that indicates the part of speech of the word given.*

5. decorous
a. verb **b.** preposition **c.** adjective **d.** noun

6. engender
a. conjunction **b.** adjective **c.** verb **d.** noun

7. machination
a. adjective **b.** interjection **c.** noun **d.** adverb

III. Spelling *Circle the word that is incorrectly spelled in each of the following groups. Then supply the correct spelling in the space given.*

8. abstruse synosure ethereal ____________

9. incongrous facade contrite ____________

10. ghoulish affront daine ____________

IV. Definition *From the list of words given below, choose the item that corresponds to each of the following definitions. Write it in the space given.*

canard	**putative**	**captious**
mesmerize	**cognizant**	**desiccated**

11. thoroughly dried out; divested of spirit or vitality; arid and uninteresting ____________

12. a false rumor, fabricated story ____________

13. aware, knowledgeable, informed ____________

14. to hypnotize; to fascinate, enthrall ____________

V. Synonym *In each of the following groups, circle the item that means the same as the* ***boldface*** *word in the introductory phrase.*

15. **engender** suspicion
   a. allay **b.** beget **c.** ridicule **d.** feign

16. the **efficacy** of the medicine
   a. nature **b.** dosage **c.** effectiveness **d.** packaging

17. an **ethereal** atmosphere
   a. infernal **b.** fetid **c.** celestial **d.** stifling

18. the **putative** reason for their failure
   a. supposed **b.** actual **c.** tragic **d.** ironic

VI. Antonym *In each of the following groups, circle the item that means the opposite of the* ***boldface*** *word in the introductory phrase.*

19. an **incongruous** combination
   a. discordant **b.** unfriendly **c.** unsuitable **d.** compatible

20. a **captious** boss
   a. cantankerous **b.** uncritical **c.** stingy **d.** strict

21. heaped **opprobrium** on them
   a. praise **b.** scorn **c.** responsibility **d.** disgrace

22. feel **contrite**
   a. angry **b.** uneasy **c.** unrepentant **d.** remorseful

---

VII. Completing the Sentence *From the list of words given below, choose the item that best completes each of the following sentences. Write it in the space given.*

facade	**decorous**	**affront**
ghoulish	**abstruse**	**desiccated**

23. A commentary was provided to help students understand some of the more ____________ ideas contained in Kant's philosophy.

24. We took fiendish delight in watching the new horror movie with its ____________ plot about strange creatures that haunt the country village.

25. The scaffolding that encircled the cathedral obstructed our view of the structure's famous Renaissance ____________.

Name ____________________

Class ____________ Date ____________ Score ____________

I. Pronunciation *Each of the following words has been divided into syllables. Place the major stress mark (′) after the syllable that is accented when the word is pronounced.*

EXAMPLE: blan dish ment ⟶ **blan′ dish ment**

1. mi nu ti ae

3. ca coph o nous

2. vi sion ar y

4. chi ca ne ry

II. Part of Speech *In each of the following groups, circle the item that indicates the part of speech of the word given.*

5. euphemism
a. verb **b.** adjective **c.** noun **d.** pronoun

6. consign
a. noun **b.** verb **c.** adverb **d.** interjection

7. beatific
a. preposition **b.** noun **c.** verb **d.** adjective

III. Spelling *Circle the word that is incorrectly spelled in each of the following groups. Then supply the correct spelling in the space given.*

8. nostrum moritorium imminent ____________

9. wizened pariah bihemath ____________

10. febril innate loath ____________

IV. Definition *From the list of words given below, choose the item that corresponds to each of the following definitions. Write it in the space given.*

coup **visionary** **gainsay**
manifest **chicanery** **blandishment**

11. a highly successful stroke, act, plan, or stratagem ____________

12. trickery, deceptive practices or tactics ____________

13. to deny, contradict; to dispute ____________

14. anything designed to flatter or coax ____________

V. Synonym

*In each of the following groups, circle the item that means the same as the **boldface** word in the introductory phrase.*

15. consign the shipment

a. order **b.** lose **c.** deliver **d.** seize

16. an **innate** ability

a. remarkable **b.** acquired **c.** athletic **d.** inherent

17. treated him like a **pariah**

a. outcast **b.** king **c.** child **d.** guest

18. imminent danger

a. remote **b.** impending **c.** terrible **d.** negligible

VI. Antonym

*In each of the following groups, circle the item that means the opposite of the **boldface** word in the introductory phrase.*

19. loath to leave

a. prepared **b.** eager **c.** reluctant **d.** unable

20. a **cacophonous** laugh

a. melodious **b.** sly **c.** hearty **d.** discordant

21. not moved by their **blandishments**

a. flattery **b.** lies **c.** appearance **d.** threats

22. declare a **moratorium**

a. postponement **b.** election **c.** escalation **d.** cessation

---

VII. Completing the Sentence

From the list of words given below, choose the item that best completes each of the following sentences. Write it in the space given.

beatific	**nostrum**	**visionary**
wizened	**coup**	**manifest**

23. A large crowd gathered around the wagon to hear the hawker tout the wondrous healing powers of his ____________________ and elixirs.

24. The doctor explained that the disease was difficult to diagnose because it ____________________ itself in such diverse ways.

25. In just a few minutes, the makeup artist had transformed the smooth face of the young actor into the ____________________ visage of an old man.

Name ______________________

Class __________ Date __________ Score __________

I. Pronunciation *Each of the following words has been divided into syllables. Place the major stress mark (′) after the syllable that is accented when the word is pronounced.*

EXAMPLE: dis si dence ⟶ **dis′ si dence**

1. a men i ty

2. pil lo ry

3. sub sist

4. prom ul gate

II. Part of Speech *In each of the following groups, circle the item that indicates the part of speech of the word given.*

5. obeisance
a. conjunction **b.** noun **c.** adjective **d.** adverb

6. mutable
a. noun **b.** adjective **c.** verb **d.** preposition

7. promulgate
a. adjective **b.** noun **c.** pronoun **d.** verb

III. Spelling *Circle the word that is incorrectly spelled in each of the following groups. Then supply the correct spelling in the space given.*

8. inviolable nasent panegyric __________

9. pittance serafic rectitude __________

10. epicurean restive apeture __________

IV. Definition *From the list of words given below, choose the item that corresponds to each of the following definitions. Write it in the space given.*

amenity **presage** **iniquity**
dissidence **improvident** **progeny**

11. a difference of opinion; discontent __________

12. wickedness, sin; a grossly immoral act __________

13. to foreshadow a future event; a warning or indication of the future __________

14. descendants, offspring, children __________

V. Synonym *In each of the following groups, circle the item that means the same as the **boldface** word in the introductory phrase.*

15. a model of **rectitude**
a. beauty **b.** probity **c.** persistence **d.** tact

16. a **restive** audience
a. attentive **b.** appreciative **c.** fidgety **d.** brilliant

17. an **inviolable** trust
a. sacred **b.** senseless **c.** childish **d.** misplaced

18. a **seraphic** smile
a. silly **b.** impish **c.** fatuous **d.** cherubic

VI. Antonym *In each of the following groups, circle the item that means the opposite of the **boldface** word in the introductory phrase.*

19. delivered a **panegyric**
a. gift **b.** diatribe **c.** baby **d.** letter

20. **epicurean** tastes
a. exotic **b.** ascetic **c.** expensive **d.** discriminating

21. a **mutable** institution
a. unchanging **b.** ancient **c.** prominent **d.** barbarous

22. received a **pittance** in return
a. reprimand **b.** trifle **c.** fortune **d.** surprise

VII. Completing the Sentence *From the list of words given below, choose the item that best completes each of the following sentences. Write it in the space given.*

presage	**pillory**	**improvident**
subsist	**dissidence**	**nascent**

23. The Impressionists, discontented because they were refused hanging space in the traditional galleries, expressed their ____________________ with separate exhibitions of their own.

24. The wilderness survival course taught us how to ____________________ on various edibles found in the forest.

25. I think it was ____________________ of him not to set aside a part of his earnings for a rainy day.

Name ______________________________

Class ______________ Date ______________ Score ______________

I. Pronunciation *Each of the following words has been divided into syllables. Place the major stress mark (′) after the syllable that is accented when the word is pronounced.*

EXAMPLE: prog e ny ⟶ **prog′ e ny**

1. mor a tor i um

2. ef fron te ry

3. in du bi ta ble

4. in vid i ous

5. se ques ter

6. fat u ous

7. im por tune

8. dis ar ray

9. sub stan tive

10. eu phe mism

11. re ful gent

12. os cil late

13. ir rep ar a ble

14. sac ri lege

15. men da cious

16. e ther e al

II. Part of Speech *In each of the following groups, circle the item that indicates the part of speech of the word given.*

17. blandishment
a. adjective **b.** noun **c.** conjunction **d.** verb

18. litany
a. noun **b.** interjection **c.** preposition **d.** adjective

19. vacillate
a. interjection **b.** verb **c.** pronoun **d.** adverb

20. decry
a. pronoun **b.** verb **c.** adverb **d.** preposition

21. diatribe
a. pronoun **b.** preposition **c.** adverb **d.** noun

22. restive
a. preposition **b.** verb **c.** adverb **d.** adjective

23. ephemeral
a. noun **b.** adjective **c.** interjection **d.** verb

24. fetish
a. noun **b.** adjective **c.** preposition **d.** verb

25. fiat
a. adverb **b.** adjective **c.** noun **d.** conjunction

26. imperturbable
a. verb **b.** conjunction **c.** adjective **d.** adverb

27. preempt
a. pronoun **b.** noun **c.** verb **d.** interjection

28. decimate
a. pronoun **b.** conjunction **c.** adjective **d.** verb

III. Spelling *Circle the word that is incorrectly spelled in each of the following groups. Then supply the correct spelling in the space given.*

29. manafest	interpolate	progeny	____________
30. mordant	beautific	furtive	____________
31. captious	onarous	portend	____________
32. wizened	omnepresent	acclamation	____________
33. misenthorp	defunct	fecund	____________
34. delineate	eclectic	vituperitive	____________
35. utopian	nuance	wrecktatude	____________
36. lumenous	illusory	moot	____________
37. rife	peremptory	mashination	____________
38. carping	abstruce	opprobrium	____________
39. belabor	presage	invilable	____________
40. perfuntory	pusillanimous	unwonted	____________

IV. Definition *From the lists of words given below, choose the item that corresponds to each of the following definitions. Write it in the space given.*

Group A

primordial	**rebuff**	**substantiate**
bastion	**overt**	**pedantry**

41. developed or created at the very beginning; going back to the most ancient times or to the earliest stage ____________

42. a fortified place, stronghold, citadel, bulwark, rampart ____________

43. to establish by evidence, prove; to give concrete form to ____________________

44. open, not hidden ____________________

Group B

jettison	**lackadaisical**	**languish**
inexorable	**figment**	**travesty**

45. a fabrication of the mind; an arbitrary notion ____________________

46. to cast overboard, get rid of as unnecessary or burdensome ____________________

47. a grotesque or grossly inferior imitation; to ridicule by imitating in a broad or burlesque way ____________________

48. lacking in spirit or interest, halfhearted ____________________

Group C

hapless	**calumniate**	**echelon**
necromancer	**bestial**	**forgo**

49. marked by the persistent absence of good fortune ____________________

50. to slander, accuse falsely or maliciously ____________________

51. to do without, abstain from, give up ____________________

52. one who claims to reveal the future through communication with the dead; a wizard ____________________

Group D

deign	**panegyric**	**ghoulish**
innate	**cacophonous**	**aperture**

53. to think it appropriate to one's dignity to do something ____________________

54. formal or elaborate praise; a tribute ____________________

55. natural, inborn, inherent; built-in ____________________

56. suggestive of someone who robs graves or otherwise preys on the dead ____________________

V. Synonym *In each of the following groups, circle the item that means the same as the **boldface** word in the introductory phrase.*

57. saw it as a deliberate **affront**
a. challenge **b.** joke **c.** compliment **d.** insult

58. the mistakes of a **neophyte**
a. rookie **b.** hero **c.** professional **d.** villain

59. **deprecate** their behavior
a. extol **b.** emulate **c.** enjoy **d.** frown upon

60. the **murky** brew
a. toxic **b.** cloudy **c.** refreshing **d.** clear

61. volunteered to **reconnoiter**
a. scout **b.** charge **c.** drill **d.** infiltrate

62. drawn into the **maelstrom**
a. whirlpool **b.** plot **c.** trap **d.** fray

63. her **laconic** style
a. concise **b.** verbose **c.** florid **d.** cryptic

64. **garnered** many awards
a. bestowed **b.** refused **c.** craved **d.** collected

65. **paroxysms** of violence
a. causes **b.** outbursts **c.** studies **d.** examples

66. change one's **raiment**
a. appearance **b.** behavior **c.** attire **d.** schedule

67. **glean** knowledge
a. esteem **b.** gather **c.** impart **d.** withhold

68. his **saturnine** expression
a. puzzled **b.** triumphant **c.** surly **d.** cheerful

69. **eschew** tradition
a. shun **b.** celebrate **c.** revere **d.** develop

70. a **wizened** visage
a. wise **b.** comical **c.** shriveled **d.** smooth

71. **pilloried** their adversaries
a. pardoned **b.** defeated **c.** betrayed **d.** ridiculed

72. **improvident** heirs
a. prudent **b.** fraudulent **c.** extravagant **d.** grieving

VI. Antonym *In each of the following groups, circle the item that means the opposite of the **boldface** word in the introductory phrase.*

73. earn a **pittance**
a. modicum **b.** salary **c.** fortune **d.** rebate

74. a sense of **propriety**
a. honor **b.** fair play **c.** unseemliness **d.** fitness

75. the **nadir** of their fortunes
a. history **b.** pinnacle **c.** low point **d.** turnaround

76. **felicitous** turns of phrase
a. elegant **b.** witty **c.** apt **d.** inappropriate

77. **attenuate** the suffering
a. worsen **b.** alleviate **c.** deplore **d.** ignore

78. the **taciturn** teenager
a. rambunctious **b.** ambitious **c.** mendacious **d.** loquacious

79. a **febrile** imagination
a. romantic **b.** relaxed **c.** feverish **d.** fertile

80. due to the storm's **propinquity**
a. course **b.** proximity **c.** distance **d.** severity

81. a **delectable** morsel
a. repulsive **b.** pungent **c.** tiny **d.** delicious

82. **irrefutable** arguments
a. clever **b.** noisy **c.** untenable **d.** lengthy

83. **impecunious** refugees
a. weary **b.** wealthy **c.** impoverished **d.** political

84. a **paltry** allowance
a. negligible **b.** gigantic **c.** minimal **d.** weekly

85. the **acuity** of her observations
a. insight **b.** fairness **c.** bias **d.** dullness

86. **decorous** behavior
a. inexplicable **b.** seemly **c.** unbecoming **d.** refined

87. a **nascent** idea
a. dying **b.** brilliant **c.** budding **d.** troublesome

88. **derelict** in their payment
a. delinquent **b.** generous **c.** erratic **d.** conscientious

VII. Completing the Sentence *From the lists of words given below, choose the item that best completes each of the following sentences. Write it in the space given.*

Group A

acquisitive	**amenity**	**verbiage**
progeny	**obtuse**	**gainsay**

89. During my stay in that primitive part of the world, I found to my surprise that I could get along quite well without many of the ____________________ of contemporary American life.

90. Even though we may find their opinions offensive, we, as Americans, cannot ____________________ their right to hold them.

91. The man is so ____________________ that I sometimes think he was born with a permanent pair of mental blinders on.

Group B

burnish	**frenetic**	**canard**
complicity	**aesthetic**	**hallow**

92. My opponent's recent insinuations that I am in the habit of stealing other people's thunder is a base ____________________, unworthy of credence.

93. Mom told me to ____________________ the bottom of the pot until she could see her face in it.

94. Since those gargoyles serve no functional purpose, I presume they were added for purely ____________________ reasons.

Group C

dissidence	**convivial**	**saturate**
peregrination	**consign**	**captious**

95. The magnificent "wandering albatross" is so named because of its extensive ____________________ over the ocean.

96. For a real bookworm like me, the library is without a doubt the most ____________________ place in the university.

97. In chemistry, a solution is said to be ____________________ when it is unable to hold any more of the material being dissolved.

Group D

stratagem	**eclectic**	**moratorium**
discomfit	**testy**	**shambles**

98. The general devised a clever ________________ to take the city, but unfortunately it backfired in our faces.

99. International efforts to prohibit the killing of whales, including a ________________ on commercial whaling, have been unable to check the depletion of some species.

100. Though I'm normally a fairly even-tempered sort of guy, I can become surprisingly ________________ when I'm tired or frustrated.

VIII. Framing Sentences (*Optional*)

On the lines provided, write an original sentence that illustrates the meaning and use of each of the following words. Do not merely reproduce one of the sentences given in the text.

101. conciliate

____

____

102. loath

____

____

103. plaintive

____

____

104. abject

____

____

105. lackadaisical

____

____

106. charlatan

107. abrogate

108. increment

109. pittance

110. mesmerize